I S.H.I.N.E.

365-Day Devotional

I S.H.I.N.E.

365-Day Devotional

Rev. Dr. Anthony D. Allen, M.Div., BCC-MH

I S.H.I.N.E. 365-Day Devotional by Rev. Dr. Anthony D. Allen, M.Div., BCC-MH

ISBN: 979-8-9901758-5-3

Printed in the United States of America
Published by Yosi Publishing, LLC
contact@yosipublishing.com | www.yosipublishing.com

Cover Design by Daria McFadgen

Disclaimer: This devotional is intended for spiritual growth, personal reflection, and emotional wellness. It is not a substitute for professional counseling, spiritual care, therapy, or medical treatment. Readers experiencing emotional distress, trauma, or mental health challenges are encouraged to seek guidance from a licensed mental health professional, pastoral counselor, or qualified healthcare provider. The insights and reflections offered are designed to complement, not replace, professional care.

Introduction

The proverb says, *"Give a man a fish, and he will eat for a day; teach a man to fish, and he will eat for a lifetime."* This wisdom underscores the importance of empowerment and self-sufficiency—equipping others with the tools to sustain spiritual care, mental wellness, and emotional balance, rather than relying on temporary solutions.

In today's fast-paced world, it's easy to neglect our inner life—the care of our mind and spirit. The purpose of this devotional is to help you cultivate a daily rhythm of spiritual renewal and mental well-being. Through Scripture-based reflections, guided prayers, and evidence-based insights, this resource invites you to grow in both faith and self-awareness.

At the heart of this devotional is the S.H.I.N.E. framework, which stands for:

- **Spiritual Growth** – Deepening your relationship with God through prayer, Word, and worship.

- **Holistic Care** – Honoring the connection between mind, body, and spirit.

- **Intentional Community** – Building relationships that encourage accountability and growth.

- **Nurturing Others** – Extending compassion, empathy, and service to those around you.

- **Emotional Resilience** – Developing strength and stability through faith, healing, and self-reflection.

Each of these five pillars serves as a foundation for the yearlong journey ahead. Every day includes a scriptural reference, reflection, and actionable application—combining biblical wisdom with practical tools grounded in psychology and wellness.

You may choose to use this devotional individually as part of your daily quiet time, alongside a journal to record your thoughts and prayers, or in a group setting to encourage shared growth and discussion. However you approach it, commit to the process with intention. Transformation happens one day, one reflection, one moment of surrender at a time.

Remember—you are not walking this path alone. God is with you in every word, every pause, and every prayer. As you move through the year, may you learn to declare with confidence: I S.H.I.N.E.!

SPIRITUAL GROWTH

Days 1–7

Weekly Prayer:

Lord, help me to clarify my intention for this journey.

Day 1: Seeking God

- **Scripture:** "You will seek me and find me when you seek me with all your heart." —Jeremiah 29:13
- **Reflection:** What does seeking God with your whole heart look like for you?
- **Application:** Spend 10 minutes praying or meditating, focusing on your desire to connect with God.

Day 2: God's Presence

- **Scripture:** "Be still, and know that I am God." — Psalm 46:10
- **Reflection:** How can stillness lead you to a deeper understanding of God?
- **Application:** Engage in a mindfulness exercise for 10 minutes, focusing on your breath.

Day 3: Trusting God

- **Scripture:** "Trust in the Lord with all your heart and lean not on your own understanding." — Proverbs 3:5-6
- **Reflection:** What areas of your life require more trust in God?
- **Application:** Write down one thing you will trust God with today.

Day 4: The Power of Prayer

- **Scripture:** "Do not be anxious about anything, but in every situation, by prayer and petition, with thanksgiving, present your requests to God." — Philippians 4:6-7

- **Reflection:** How does prayer alleviate anxiety?

- **Application:** Create a prayer journal and write your prayers today.

Day 5: Gratitude

- **Scripture:** "Rejoice always, pray continually, give thanks in all circumstances." — 1 Thessalonians 5:16-18

- **Reflection:** How does gratitude impact your spiritual life?

- **Practice:** List five things you are grateful for today.

Day 6: Scripture Meditation

- **Scripture:** "Keep this Book of the Law always on your lips; meditate on it day and night." — Joshua 1:8

- **Reflection:** How can meditating on scripture deepen your faith?

- **Application:** Choose a verse to meditate on throughout the day.

Day 7: Community in Faith

- **Scripture:** "And let us consider how we may spur one another on toward love and good deeds." — Hebrews 10:24-25
- **Reflection:** What role does community play in your spiritual growth?
- **Application:** Reach out to a friend or family member for a spiritual conversation.

Days 8–14

Weekly Prayer:

Help me to know myself deeply and truthfully.

Day 8: Worship

- **Scripture:** "God is spirit, and his worshipers must worship in the Spirit and in truth." — John 4:24
- **Reflection:** What does true worship mean to you?
- **Application:** Spend time in worship through music or art.

Day 9: Serving Others

- **Scripture:** "Serve one another humbly in love." — Galatians 5:13
- **Reflection:** How does serving others enhance your spiritual journey?
- **Application:** Volunteer for a local charity or help someone in need.

Day 10: Reflecting on Your Journey

- **Scripture:** "I will remember the deeds of the Lord; yes, I will remember your miracles of long ago." — Psalm 77:11-12
- **Reflection:** How can reflecting on past experiences strengthen your faith?
- **Application:** Write about a significant moment in your spiritual journey.

Day 11: The Importance of Silence

- **Scripture:** "The Lord is in his holy temple; let all the earth be silent before him." — Habakkuk 2:20
- **Reflection:** What do you learn in

silence?

- **Application:** Spend time in silence, listening for God's voice.

Day 12: Faith in Action

- **Scripture:** "Faith by itself, if it is not accompanied by action, is dead." — James 2:17
- **Reflection:** How can you put your faith into action today?
- **Application:** Identify one action step that reflects your faith.

Day 13: The Role of the Holy Spirit

- **Scripture**: "But the Advocate, the Holy Spirit, whom the Father will send in my name, will teach you all things." — John 14:26
- **Reflection:** How does the Holy Spirit guide you?
- **Application:** Pray for guidance from the Holy Spirit in a specific area of your life.

Day 14: Finding Peace

- **Scripture:** "Peace I leave with you; my peace I give you." —John 14:27
- **Reflection:** How can you cultivate peace in your life?
- **Application:** Engage in a calming activity, such as deep breathing or stretching.

Days 15–21

Weekly Prayer:

Teach me to accept myself fully and unconditionally.

Day 15: Facing Doubt

- **Scripture:** "I do believe; help me overcome my unbelief!" — Mark 9:24
- **Reflection:** How can you confront your doubts?
- **Application:** Write about a doubt you're facing and pray for strength.

Day 16: Embracing Forgiveness

- **Scripture:** "Be kind and compassionate to one another, forgiving each other, just as in Christ God forgave you." — Ephesians 4:32
- **Reflection:** What does forgiveness mean in your life?
- **Application:** Write a letter of forgiveness to yourself or someone (you don't need to send it).

Day 17: The Value of Patience

- **Scripture:** "Be joyful in hope, patient in affliction, faithful in prayer." — Romans 12:12
- **Reflection:** How can patience strengthen your faith?
- **Application:** Identify an area where you need to practice patience.

Day 18: God's Promises

- **Scripture:** "He has given us his very

great and precious promises."

- **Reflection:** Which of God's promises do you hold onto? — 2 Peter 1:4
- **Application:** Write down God's promises that resonate with you.

Day 19: The Importance of Hope

- **Scripture:** "May the God of hope fill you with all joy and peace as you trust in him." — Romans 15:13
- **Reflection:** How does hope influence your spiritual growth?
- **Application:** List three things you hope for in the future.

Day 20: Finding Strength in Weakness

- **Scripture:** "My grace is sufficient for you, for my power is made perfect in weakness." — 2 Corinthians 12:9
- **Reflection:** How can your weaknesses lead to growth?

- **Application**: Share a weakness with a trusted friend and discuss it.

Day 21: The Gift of Grace

- **Scripture:** "For it is by grace you have been saved, through faith." — Ephesians 2:8-9
- **Reflection:** How does understanding grace change your perspective?
- **Application:** Reflect on a time you experienced grace.

Days 21–28

Weekly Prayer:

Send me the guidance I need on my spiritual path.

Day 22: Daily Devotion

- **Scripture:** "Your word is a lamp for my feet, a light on my path."
- **Reflection:** How can daily devotionals guide your life? — Psalm 119:105
- **Application:** Start a daily reading plan for the next week.

Day 23: Fasting

- **Scripture:** "When you fast, do not look somber as the hypocrites do." — Matthew 6:16-18
- **Reflection:** What can fasting teach you about dependence on God?
- **Application:** Choose a day to fast from something (food, social media) and focus on prayer.

Day 24: Journaling

- **Scripture:** "I will consider all your works and meditate on all your mighty deeds." — Psalm 77:12
- **Reflection:** How can journaling enhance your spiritual journey?
- **Application:** Write a journal entry reflecting on God's works in your life.

Day 25: Affirmations of Faith

- **Scripture:** "I can do all this through him who gives me strength." — Philippians

4:13

- **Reflection:** How can affirmations strengthen your faith?

- **Application:** Create a list of affirmations to repeat daily.

Day 26: The Role of Silence and Solitude

- **Scripture:** "Very early in the morning, while it was still dark, Jesus got up, left the house and went off to a solitary place." — Mark 1:35

- **Reflection:** How does solitude help you connect with God?

- **Application:** Spend an hour in solitude, reflecting on your relationship with God.

Day 27: The Power of Praise

- **Scripture:** "Enter his gates with thanksgiving and his courts with praise." — Psalm 100:4

- **Reflection:** How does praise change

your perspective?

- **Application:** Create a playlist of worship songs and spend time in praise.

Day 28: Living Out Your Faith

Scripture: "Whatever you do, work at it with all your heart." — Colossians 3:23

Reflection: How can you live out your faith in everyday activities?

Application: Choose one task today to do with a spirit of service.

Days 29–35

Weekly Prayer:

I surrender my worries and fears to you, trusting in your plan.

Day 29: Resilience Through Trials

- **Scripture:** "Consider it pure joy, my brothers and sisters, whenever you face trials of many kinds." — James 1:2-4

- **Reflection:** How can trials lead to growth?

- **Application:** Reflect on a trial that strengthened your faith.

Day 30: The Importance of Fellowship

- **Scripture:** "They devoted themselves to the apostles' teaching and to fellowship." — Acts 2:42

- **Reflection:** How does fellowship enrich your spiritual life?

- **Application:** Attend a church service or small group this week.

Day 31: Spiritual Gifts

- **Scripture:** "Each of you should use whatever gift you have received to serve others." — 1 Peter 4:10

- **Reflection:** What are your spiritual gifts?

- **Application:** Identify and use one of your gifts to serve someone this week.

Day 32: The Importance of Reflection

- **Scripture:** "Let us examine our ways and

test them, and let us return to the Lord." — Lamentations 3:40

- **Reflection:** How can reflection lead to spiritual growth?
- **Application:** Set aside time for self-examination and prayer.

Day 33: Living with Purpose

- **Scripture:** "For we are God's handiwork, created in Christ Jesus to do good works." — Ephesians 2:10
- **Reflection:** What is your purpose in God's plan?
- **Application:** Write down your life purpose statement.

Day 34: Embracing Change

- **Scripture:** "See, I am doing a new thing!" — Isaiah 43:19
- **Reflection:** How can embracing change lead to growth?
- **Application:** Identify an area of your life

where you need to embrace change.

Day 35: The Beauty of Creation

- **Scripture:** "The heavens declare the glory of God; the skies proclaim the work of his hands." — Psalm 19:1

- **Reflection:** How does nature reflect God's glory?

- **Application:** Spend time outdoors and observe the beauty of creation.

Days 36–42

Weekly Prayer:

Help me reflect on my spiritual journey thus far.

Day 36: The Importance of Faith

- **Scripture:** "Now faith is confidence in what we hope for and assurance about what we do not see." — Hebrews 11:1
- **Reflection:** How does faith shape your perspective?
- **Application:** Write about a situation where you need to exercise faith.

Day 37: The Role of Hope

- **Scripture:** "Hope does not put us to shame." — Romans 5:5
- **Reflection:** How does hope influence your daily life?
- **Application:** Reflect on a hope you have for the future.

Day 38: The Gift of Love

- **Scripture:** "And now these three remain: faith, hope, and love. But the greatest of these is love." — 1 Corinthians 13:13
- **Reflection:** How can love be a guiding principle in your life?
- **Application:** Perform an act of kindness for someone today.

Day 39: The Importance of Rest

- **Scripture:** "Come to me, all you who are weary and burdened, and I will give you rest." — Matthew 11:28
- **Reflection:** How does rest rejuvenate

your spirit?

- **Application:** Set aside time for rest and reflection today.

Day 40: The Power of Story

- **Scripture:** "We will tell the next generation the praiseworthy deeds of the Lord." — Psalm 78:4
- **Reflection:** How can sharing your story inspire others?
- **Application:** Share your testimony with someone this week.

Day 41: The Importance of Discipline

- **Scripture:** "Run in such a way as to get the prize." — 1 Corinthians 9:24–27
- **Reflection:** How does discipline impact your spiritual growth?
- **Application:** Set a spiritual discipline goal for the month.

Day 42: Spiritual Warfare

- **Scripture:** "For our struggle is not against flesh and blood." — Ephesians 6:12
- **Reflection:** How can you prepare for spiritual challenges?
- **Application:** Pray for protection and strength against spiritual battles.

Days 43–49

Weekly Prayer:

I commit to this journey of spiritual growth.

Day 43: The Call to Action

- **Scripture:** "Let your light shine before others." — Matthew 5:16
- **Reflection:** How can you be a light in your community?
- **Application:** Identify one way you can serve your community this week.

Day 44: The Importance of Listening

- **Scripture:** "Everyone should be quick to

listen, slow to speak."

- **Reflection:** How can listening enhance your relationships? —James 1:19
- **Application:** Practice active listening in your next conversation.

Day 45: The Role of Faith in Trials

- **Scripture:** "And we know that in all things God works for the good of those who love him." — Romans 8:28
- **Reflection:** How can you find hope in difficult times?
- **Application:** Write about a trial and how it has shaped your faith.

Day 46: The Importance of Accountability

- **Scripture:** "As iron sharpens iron, so one person sharpens another." — Proverbs 27:17
- **Reflection:** Who holds you accountable in your spiritual journey?

- **Application:** Reach out to an accountability partner.

Day 47: The Power of Testimony

- **Scripture:** "They triumphed over him by the blood of the Lamb and by the word of their testimony." — Revelation 12:11
- **Reflection:** How can sharing your testimony encourage others?
- **Application:** Write your testimony and share it with someone.

Day 48: The Importance of Faithfulness

- **Scripture:** "Now it is required that those who have been given a trust must prove faithful." — 1 Corinthians 4:2
- **Reflection:** How can you be faithful in your commitments?
- **Application:** Reflect on your commitments and how you can fulfill them.

Day 49: The Call to Forgiveness

- **Scripture:** "Forgive as the Lord forgave you." — Colossians 3:13
- **Reflection:** What does forgiveness mean in your relationships?
- **Application:** Identify someone you need to forgive and pray for them.

DAYS 50–56

Weekly Prayer:

Grant me wisdom to understand your teachings.

Day 50: Reflecting on Your Journey

- **Scripture:** "Search me, God, and know my heart; test me and know my anxious thoughts." — Psalm 139:23-24
- **Reflection:** How have you grown in your spiritual journey?
- **Application:** Write a letter to God reflecting on your journey so far.

Day 51: The Importance of Hope

- **Scripture:** "For I know the plans I have for you." —Jeremiah 29:11
- **Reflection:** How does hope shape your future?
- **Application:** Write down a hope you have for the future and pray for it.

Day 52: The Gift of Community

- **Scripture:** "If we walk in the light, as he is in the light, we have fellowship with one another." — 1 John 1:7
- **Reflection:** How does community support your spiritual growth?
- **Application:** Attend a community or church event this week.

Day 53: Living with Intention

- **Scripture:** "Whatever you do, work at it with all your heart." — Colossians 3:23
- **Reflection:** How can you live intentionally in your daily life?

- **Application:** Set specific intentions for the upcoming week.

Day 54: The Role of Gratitude

- **Scripture:** "Give thanks to the Lord, for he is good." — Psalm 107:1
- **Reflection:** How does gratitude change your perspective?
- **Application:** Keep a gratitude journal for the next week.

Day 55: The Importance of Sharing

- **Scripture:** "It is more blessed to give than to receive." — Acts 20:35
- **Reflection:** How can sharing your resources bless others?
- **Application:** Identify something you can share with someone in need.

Day 56: Embracing God's Love

- **Scripture:** "But God demonstrates his own love for us in this: While we were still sinners, Christ died for us." —

Romans 5:8

- **Reflection:** How does understanding God's love impact your life?
- **Application:** Spend time in prayer, reflecting on God's love for you.

Days 57–63

Weekly Prayer:

Teach me to embrace my imperfections and learn from them.

Day 57: The Power of Hope

- **Scripture:** "May the God of hope fill you with all joy and peace."
- **Reflection:** How can hope to sustain you during difficult times? — Romans 15:13
- **Application:** Write down three sources of hope in your life.

Day 58: The Importance of Faith

- **Scripture:** "And without faith, it is impossible to please God." — Hebrews 11:6
- **Reflection:** How can you strengthen your faith in God?
- **Application:** Identify an area where you want to grow in faith.

Day 59: Reflecting on God's Goodness

- **Scripture:** "For the Lord is good and his love endures forever." — Psalm 100:5
- **Reflection:** How have you experienced God's goodness in your life?
- **Application:** Write a letter to God expressing your gratitude for His goodness.

Day 60: The Call to Action

- **Scripture:** "Therefore, go and make disciples of all nations."

- **Reflection:** How can you share your faith with others? — Matthew 28:19-20

- **Application:** Plan a way to share your faith story with someone this week.

Day 61: Embracing New Beginnings

- **Scripture:** "See, I am doing a new thing!" — Isaiah 43:19

- **Reflection:** What new beginnings is God calling you to?

- **Application:** Identify one new beginning you want to embrace.

Day 62: The Importance of Rest

- **Scripture:** "On the seventh day he rested." — Exodus 31:17

- **Reflection:** How does rest contribute to spiritual growth?

- **Application:** Schedule a day of rest and reflection.

Day 63: The Role of Faithfulness

- **Scripture:** "Well done, good and faithful servant!" — Matthew 25:21
- **Reflection:** How can you be more faithful in your responsibilities?
- **Application:** Identify one area where you can demonstrate faithfulness.

DAYS 64–73

Weekly Prayer:

Thank you for the blessings in my life; help me recognize them.

Day 64: The Gift of Peace

- **Scripture:** "Peace I leave with you; my peace I give you." —John 14:27
- **Reflection:** How can you cultivate peace in your life?
- **Application:** Engage in a calming activity, such as meditation or nature walks.

Day 65: The Importance of Listening

- **Scripture:** "To answer before listening—that is folly and shame." — Proverbs 18:13
- **Reflection:** How can listening improve your relationships?
- **Application:** Practice active listening in your next conversation.

Day 66: The Call to Serve

- **Scripture:** "The Son of Man did not come to be served, but to serve." — Matthew 20:28
- **Reflection:** How can you follow Jesus' example of service?
- **Application:** Offer your help to someone in your community.

Day 67: The Importance of Community

- **Scripture:** "So in Christ we, though many, form one body." — Romans 12:5

- **Reflection:** How does the community support your spiritual growth?
- **Application:** Attend a community or church event this week.

Day 68: Reflecting on Your Journey

- **Scripture:** "Search me, God, and know my heart." — Psalm 139:23-24
- **Reflection:** How have you grown in your spiritual journey?
- **Application:** Write a letter to God reflecting on your journey.

Day 69: Embracing God's Love

- **Scripture:** "This is how God showed his love among us: He sent his one and only Son." — 1 John 4:9
- **Reflection:** How does understanding God's love impact your life?
- **Application:** Spend time in prayer, reflecting on God's love for you.

Day 70: The Importance of Hope

- **Scripture:** "The steadfast love of the Lord never ceases; his mercies never come to an end." — Lamentations 3:22-23
- **Reflection:** How does hope sustain you during difficult times?
- **Application:** Write down three sources of hope in your life.

Day 71: The Call to Action

- **Scripture:** "Let your light shine before others." — Matthew 5:16
- **Reflection:** How can you be a light in your community?
- **Application:** Identify one way you can serve your community this week.

Day 72: Embracing New Beginnings

- **Scripture:** "See, I am doing a new thing!" — Isaiah 43:19
- **Reflection:** What new beginnings is

God calling you to?

- **Application:** Identify one new beginning you want to embrace.

Day 73: Conclusion and Commitment

- **Scripture:** "Forgetting what is behind and straining toward what is ahead." — Philippians 3:13-14
- **Reflection:** What commitments will you make moving forward in your spiritual journey?
- **Application:** Write a commitment statement for your spiritual growth.

HOLISTIC CARE

Days 74–80

Weekly Prayer:

Lord, help me to clarify my intention for this journey.

Day 74: Spiritual Awareness

- **Scripture:** "Be still, and know that I am God." — Psalm 46:10
- **Reflection:** Embrace moments of stillness to connect with God.
- **Application:** Spend five minutes in silence today. Focus on your breath and invite peace into your heart.

Day 75: Mental Clarity

- **Scripture:** “Do not conform to the pattern of this world, but be transformed by the renewing of your mind.” — Romans 12:2

- **Reflection:** Renewing the mind is essential for holistic health.

- **Application:** Identify one negative thought pattern and replace it with a positive affirmation.

Day 76: Emotional Healing

- **Scripture:** - “The Lord is close to the brokenhearted and saves those who are crushed in spirit.” — Psalm 34:18

- **Reflection:** Acknowledge your emotions; it’s okay to feel.

- **Application:** Journal about your feelings today. Write down what’s on your heart.

Day 77: Social Connection

- **Scripture:** "Two are better than one, because they have a good return for their labor." — Ecclesiastes 4:9-10
- **Reflection:** Relationships are vital for emotional and mental health.
- **Application:** Reach out to a friend or family member today. Share a meal or simply talk.

Day 78: Physical Well-being

- **Scripture:** "Your bodies are temples of the Holy Spirit." — 1 Corinthians 6:19-20
- **Reflection:** Caring for your body honors God.
- **Application:** Drink at least 8 glasses of water today to stay hydrated.

Day 79: Spiritual Growth

- **Scripture:** "But grow in the grace and knowledge of our Lord and Savior Jesus

Christ." — 2 Peter 3:18

- **Reflection:** Growth is a lifelong journey.
- **Application:** Read a chapter from the Bible today and reflect on its meaning.

Day 80: Mental Resilience

- **Scripture:** "I can do all things through Christ who strengthens me." — Philippians 4:13
- **Reflection:** Mental resilience is built through faith and practice.
- **Application:** Identify a challenge you face and pray for strength and wisdom.

DAYS 81–87

Weekly Prayer:

Help me to know myself deeply and truthfully.

Day 81: Emotional Expression

- **Scripture:** "In your anger do not sin; do not let the sun go down while you are still angry." — Ephesians 4:26
- **Reflection:** Managing emotions is crucial for holistic health.
- **Application:** Practice a breathing exercise when you feel overwhelmed.

Day 82: Social Support

- **Scripture:** "Carry each other's burdens, and in this way you will fulfill the law of Christ." — Galatians 6:2
- **Reflection:** Supporting others strengthens community.
- **Application:** Offer help to someone in need today.

Day 83: Physical Activity

- **Scripture:** "For physical training is of some value, but godliness has value for all things." — 1 Timothy 4:8
- **Reflection:** Balance is key in physical and spiritual training.
- **Application:** Engage in at least 30 minutes of physical activity today.

Day 84: Spiritual Reflection

- **Scripture:** "The Lord is good to those who hope in him, to the one who seeks him." — Lamentations 3:25

- **Reflection:** Hope is a powerful motivator.
- **Application:** Create a vision board that reflects your hopes and dreams.

Day 85: Mental Focus

- **Scripture:** "Set your minds on things that are above, not on things that are on earth." — Colossians 3:2
- **Reflection:** Focus on what truly matters.
- **Application:** Spend 10 minutes meditating on a positive scripture today.

Day 86: Emotional Balance

- **Scripture:** "A happy heart makes the face cheerful." — Proverbs 15:13
- **Reflection:** Joy is a choice we can make daily.
- **Application:** List three things that bring you joy and engage in one today.

Day 87: Social Engagement

- **Scripture:** "And let us consider how we may spur one another on toward love and good deeds." — Hebrews 10:24-25
- **Reflection:** Encouragement is vital in community.
- **Application:** Send a note of encouragement to someone today.

Days 88–94

Weekly Prayer:

Teach me to accept myself fully and unconditionally.

Day 88: Physical Nutrition

- **Scripture:** "I give you every seed-bearing plant on the face of the whole earth and every tree that has fruit." — Genesis 1:29
- **Reflection:** Nourishment comes from God's creation.
- **Application:** Prepare a healthy meal using whole foods today.

Day 89: Spiritual Community

- **Scripture:** "For where two or three gather in my name, there am I with them." — Matthew 18:20
- **Reflection:** Community enhances spiritual growth.
- **Application:** Join a small group or attend a church service this week.

Day 90: Mental Self-Care

- **Scripture:** "Cast all your anxiety on him because he cares for you. — 1 Peter 5:7
- **Reflection:** Self-care is essential for mental health.
- **Application:** Practice a self-care activity today, such as reading or taking a bath.

Day 91: Emotional Awareness

- **Scripture:** "Everyone should be quick to listen, slow to speak and slow to become angry." —James 1:19
- **Reflection:** Listening is a powerful tool

for emotional health.

- **Application:** Practice active listening in your conversations today.

Day 92: Social Responsibility

- **Scripture:** "Whatever you did for one of the least of these brothers and sisters of mine, you did for me." — Matthew 25:40
- **Reflection:** Serving others is serving God.
- **Application:** Volunteer for a local charity or help a neighbor in need.

Day 93: Physical Rest

- **Scripture:** "Remember the Sabbath day by keeping it holy." — Exodus 20:8
- **Reflection:** Rest is a commandment for our health.
- **Application:** Dedicate a day to rest and rejuvenate this week.

Day 94: Spiritual Discernment

- **Scripture:** "Trust in the Lord with all your heart and lean not on your own understanding." — Proverbs 3:5-6
- **Reflection:** Trusting God leads to clarity.
- **Application:** Pray for guidance in a decision you need to make.

Days 95–101

Weekly Prayer:

Send me the guidance I need on my spiritual path.

Day 95: Mental Organization

- **Scripture:** "But everything should be done in a fitting and orderly way." — 1 Corinthians 14:40
- **Reflection:** Organization reduces stress.
- **Application:** Spend 15 minutes decluttering a space in your home.

Day 96: Emotional Release

- **Scripture:** "Come to me, all you who are weary and burdened, and I will give you rest." — Matthew 11:28
- **Reflection:** Jesus invites us to release our burdens.
- **Application:** Identify a burden you can release to God today through prayer.

Day 97: Social Gratitude

- **Scripture:** "Give thanks in all circumstances; for this is God's will for you in Christ Jesus." — 1 Thessalonians 5:18
- **Reflection:** Gratitude strengthens relationships.
- **Application:** Write a thank-you note to someone who has impacted your life.

Day 98: Physical Movement

- **Scripture:** "That each of them may eat and drink, and find satisfaction in all their toil—this is the gift of God." — Ecclesiastes 3:13

- **Reflection:** Movement is a gift that enhances life.

- **Application:** Go for a walk in nature today, appreciating God's creation.

Day 99: Spiritual Reflection

- **Scripture:** "Your word is a lamp for my feet, a light on my path." — Psalm 119:105

- **Reflection:** Scripture guides us in our journey.

- **Application:** Meditate on a verse today and reflect on its application in your life.

Day 100: Mental Empowerment

- **Scripture:** "But those who hope in the Lord will renew their strength." — Isaiah 40:31

- **Reflection:** Empowerment comes from faith.

- **Application:** Identify a personal strength and use it to face a challenge today.

Day 101: Emotional Honesty

- **Scripture:** "I praise you because I am fearfully and wonderfully made." — Psalm 139:14
- **Reflection:** Embrace your uniqueness.
- **Application:** Write down three things you appreciate about yourself.

Days 102–108

Weekly Prayer:

I surrender my worries and fears to you, trusting in your plan.

Day 102: Social Kindness

- **Scripture:** "Those who are kind benefit themselves, but the cruel bring ruin on themselves." — Proverbs 11:17

- **Reflection:** Kindness is a powerful force in relationships.

- **Application:** Perform a random act of kindness today.

Day 103: Physical Balance

- **Scripture:** "Let your gentleness be evident to all. The Lord is near." — Philippians 4:5
- **Reflection:** Balance in life promotes overall health.
- **Application:** Practice yoga or stretching for 20 minutes today.

Day 104: Spiritual Hope

- **Scripture:** "For I know the plans I have for you, declares the Lord." — Jeremiah 29:11
- **Reflection:** Hope in God's plans brings peace.
- **Application:** Write down your hopes for the future and pray over them.

Day 105: Mental Clarity

- **Scripture:** "For the Lord gives wisdom; from his mouth come knowledge and understanding." — Proverbs 2:6

- **Reflection:** Seek wisdom in all decisions.
- **Application:** Read a book or article that challenges your thinking today.

Day 106: Emotional Support

- **Scripture:** "Who comforts us in all our troubles, so that we can comfort those in any trouble." — 2 Corinthians 1:4
- **Reflection:** Our experiences can help others.
- **Application:** Share your story with someone who may benefit from it.

Day 107: Social Engagement

- **Scripture:** "Be devoted to one another in love. Honor one another above yourselves." — Romans 12:10
- **Reflection:** Devotion to others strengthens community.
- **Application:** Plan a gathering with friends or family this week.

Day 108: Physical Health

- **Scripture:** "Do not be wise in your own eyes; fear the Lord and shun evil. This will bring health to your body and nourishment to your bones." — Proverbs 3:7–8
- **Reflection:** Wisdom leads to health.
- **Application:** Make a healthy meal choice today, focusing on nutrition.

DAYS 109–115

Weekly Prayer:

Help me reflect on my spiritual journey thus far.

Day 109: Spiritual Reflection

- **Scripture:** "I have hidden your word in my heart that I might not sin against you." — Psalm 119:11
- **Reflection:** Internalizing scripture strengthens our faith.
- **Application:** Memorize a verse that speaks to you.

Day 110: Mental Growth

- **Scripture:** "The heart of the discerning acquires knowledge, for the ears of the wise seek it out." — Proverbs 18:15
- **Reflection:** Knowledge is a lifelong pursuit.
- **Application:** Attend a workshop or seminar that interests you.

Day 111: Emotional Self-Care

- **Scripture:** "May your whole spirit, soul, and body be kept blameless at the coming of our Lord Jesus Christ." — 1 Thessalonians 5:23
- **Reflection:** Holistic care includes all aspects of our being.
- **Application:** Set aside time for an activity that nourishes your spirit today.

Day 112: Social Awareness

- **Scripture:** "Not looking to your own interests but each of you to the interests of the others." — Philippians 2:4

- **Reflection:** Awareness of others fosters compassion.
- **Application:** Volunteer your time to help a local charity today.

Day 113: Physical Activity

- **Scripture:** "There is a time for everything, and a season for every activity under the heavens." — Ecclesiastes 3:1
- **Reflection:** Balance is essential in our activities.
- **Application:** Schedule regular physical activity into your week.

Day 114: Spiritual Guidance

- **Scripture:** "Show me your ways, Lord, teach me your paths. Guide me in your truth and teach me." — Psalm 25:4-5
- **Reflection:** Seeking guidance is vital for spiritual growth.

- **Application:** Spend time in prayer, asking for guidance in your life.

Day 115: Mental Clarity

- **Scripture:** "Turning your ear to wisdom and applying your heart to understanding." — Proverbs 2:2
- **Reflection:** Clarity comes from seeking understanding.
- **Application:** Take time to reflect on a personal challenge and seek clarity through prayer.

Days 116–122

Weekly Prayer:

I commit to this journey of spiritual growth.

Day 116: Emotional Connection

- **Scripture:** "We love because he first loved us." — 1 John 4:19
- **Reflection:** Our capacity to love is rooted in God's love for us.
- **Application:** Reach out to someone you care about and express your love for them.

Day 117: Social Responsibility

- **Scripture:** "To whom much is given, much will be required." — Luke 12:48
- **Reflection:** We are called to use our resources to help others.
- **Application:** Donate to a cause that resonates with you.

Day 118: Physical Restoration

- **Scripture:** "He gives strength to the weary and increases the power of the weak." — Isaiah 40:29
- **Reflection:** Restoration comes from God.
- **Application:** Take a day to rest and recharge, focusing on self-care.

Day 119: Spiritual Assurance

- **Scripture:** "For I am convinced that neither death nor life, neither angels nor demons, neither the present nor the future, nor any powers…" — Romans

8:38-39

- **Reflection:** Nothing can separate us from God's love.
- **Application:** Reflect on God's love in your life and write down your thoughts.

Day 120: Mental Awareness

- **Scripture:** "Above all else, guard your heart, for everything you do flows from it." — Proverbs 4:23
- **Reflection:** Protecting our mental health is vital.
- **Application:** Identify a mental health boundary you need to establish.

Day 121: Emotional Resilience

- **Scripture:** "For God has not given us a spirit of fear, but of power, love, and self-discipline." — 2 Timothy 1:7
- **Reflection:** Resilience is a gift from God.
- **Application:** Identify a fear and take a

small step to confront it today.

Day 122: Social Connection

- **Scripture:** "As iron sharpens iron, so one person sharpens another." — Proverbs 27:17
- **Reflection:** Relationships help us grow.
- **Application:** Schedule a time to meet with a mentor or friend who encourages you.

Days 123–129

Weekly Prayer:

Teach me to embrace my imperfections and learn from them.

Day 123: Physical Activity

- **Scripture:** "Do you not know that in a race all the runners run, but only one gets the prize?" — 1 Corinthians 9:24
- **Reflection:** Discipline in physical activity yields rewards.
- **Application:** Set a fitness goal for the week and work towards it.

Day 124: Spiritual Reflection

- **Scripture:** "Your word is a lamp for my feet, a light on my path." — Psalm 119:105
- **Reflection:** Scripture provides guidance in our journey.
- **Application:** Reflect on a scripture that has guided you and share its impact.

Day 125: Mental Empowerment

- **Scripture:** "Now to him who is able to do immeasurably more than all we ask or imagine…" — Ephesians 3:20
- **Reflection:** God empowers us to achieve great things.
- **Application:** Set a personal goal that stretches your abilities.

Day 126: Emotional Honesty

- **Scripture:** "Anxiety weighs down the heart, but a kind word cheers it up." — Proverbs 12:25

- **Reflection:** Honesty about feelings fosters healing.
- **Application:** Share your feelings with a trusted friend or family member.

Day 127: Social Engagement

- **Scripture:** "We who are strong ought to bear with the failings of the weak and not to please ourselves." — Romans 15:1
- **Reflection:** Supporting others strengthens community.
- **Application:** Offer support to someone who is struggling today.

Day 128: Physical Nutrition

- **Scripture:** "So whether you eat or drink or whatever you do, do it all for the glory of God." — 1 Corinthians 10:31
- **Reflection:** Nutrition is a form of worship.
- **Application:** Prepare a meal that honors your body and reflects gratitude.

Day 129: Spiritual Growth

- **Scripture:** "Therefore, since we are surrounded by such a great cloud of witnesses..." — Hebrews 12:1
- **Reflection:** Growth is a journey supported by others.
- **Application:** Reflect on the people who have influenced your faith journey.

Days 130–136

Weekly Prayer:

Teach me to embrace my imperfections and learn from them.

Day 130: Mental Clarity

- **Scripture:** "Finally, brothers and sisters, whatever is true, whatever is noble, whatever is right…" — Philippians 4:8
- **Reflection:** Focus on positive thoughts.
- **Application:** Write down three positive thoughts to meditate on today.

Day 131: Emotional Connection

- **Scripture:** "Above all, love each other deeply, because love covers over a multitude of sins." — 1 Peter 4:8
- **Reflection:** Deep connections are built on love.
- **Application:** Reach out to someone you haven't spoken to in a while.

Day 132: Social Responsibility

- **Scripture:** "Let your light shine before others, that they may see your good deeds…" — Matthew 5:16
- **Reflection:** Our actions can inspire others.
- **Application:** Perform a good deed today without seeking recognition.

Day 133: Physical Activity

- **Scripture:** "Dear friend, I pray that you may enjoy good health and that all may go well with you…" — 3 John 1:2

- **Reflection:** Health is a blessing.
- **Application:** Engage in a physical activity that brings you joy today.

Day 134: Spiritual Reflection

- **Scripture:** "I will meditate on your precepts and consider your ways." — Psalm 119:15
- **Reflection:** Meditation deepens our understanding of God.
- **Application:** Spend time meditating on a specific passage or concept.

Day 135: Mental Empowerment

- **Scripture:** "We demolish arguments and every pretension that sets itself up against the knowledge of God…" — 2 Corinthians 10:5
- **Reflection:** Empower your mind with truth.
- **Application:** Challenge a negative belief today with a truth from scripture.

Day 136: Emotional Healing

- **Scripture:** "He heals the brokenhearted and binds up their wounds." — Psalm 147:3
- **Reflection:** Healing is a process that God supports.
- **Application:** Identify an area of emotional pain and pray for healing.

Days 137–146

Weekly Prayer:

Thank you for the blessings in my life; help me recognize them.

Day 137: Social Connection

- **Scripture:** "And let us consider how we may spur one another on toward love and good deeds." — Hebrews 10:24
- **Reflection:** Encouragement is vital in relationships.
- **Application:** Send a message to encourage someone today.

Day 138: Physical Health

- **Scripture:** "Do you not know that your bodies are temples of the Holy Spirit?" — 1 Corinthians 6:19
- **Reflection:** Caring for our bodies is an act of worship.
- **Application:** Choose a healthy snack today to honor your body.

Day 139: Spiritual Awareness

- **Scripture:** "God is spirit, and his worshipers must worship in the Spirit and in truth." — John 4:24
- **Reflection:** True worship comes from the heart.
- **Application:** Spend time in worship today, expressing your love for God.

Day 140: Mental Clarity

- **Scripture:** "Let the wise listen and add to their learning…" — Proverbs 1:5
- **Reflection:** Wisdom is a continuous

journey.

- **Application:** Seek a mentor or teacher to learn from this week.

Day 141: Emotional Expression

- **Scripture:** "Be kind and compassionate to one another, forgiving each other, just as in Christ God forgave you." — Ephesians 4:32
- **Reflection:** Compassion fosters emotional health.
- **Application:** Practice forgiveness towards someone today.

Day 142: Social Responsibility

- **Scripture:** "Do to others as you would have them do to you." — Luke 6:31
- **Reflection:** The Golden Rule guides our interactions.
- **Application:** Treat someone today as you wish to be treated.

Day 143: Physical Well-being

- **Scripture:** "For physical training is of some value, but godliness has value for all things." — 1 Timothy 4:8
- **Reflection:** Balance physical and spiritual training.
- **Application:** Create a balanced meal plan for the week.

Day 144: Spiritual Reflection

- **Scripture:** "If any of you lacks wisdom, you should ask God…" — James 1:5
- **Reflection:** Seeking wisdom is a sign of humility.
- **Application:** Spend time in prayer asking for wisdom in a specific area of your life.

Day 145: Mental Resilience

- **Scripture:** "Be joyful in hope, patient in affliction, faithful in prayer." — Romans 12:12

- **Reflection:** Resilience is built through faith and perseverance.
- **Application:** Identify a challenge and commit to prayerfully facing it this week.

Day 146: Holistic Integration

- **Scripture:** "May God himself, the God of peace, sanctify you through and through." — 1 Thessalonians 5:23
- **Reflection:** Holistic health encompasses spirit, mind, and body.
- **Application:** Reflect on the areas of your life that need more balance and commit to a plan for holistic care moving forward.

INTENTIONAL COMMUNITY

Days 147–153

Weekly Prayer:

Lord, help me to clarify my intention for this journey.

Day 147: The Foundation of Community

- **Scripture:** "All the believers were together and had everything in common." — Acts 2:44–47
- **Reflection:** Community thrives on shared values and purpose.
- **Application:** Write down what you value most in community and share it with a group member.

Day 148: The Power of Unity

- **Scripture:** "How good and pleasant it is when God's people live together in unity!" — Psalm 133:1
- **Reflection:** Unity strengthens our bonds and enhances our impact.
- **Application:** Plan a group activity that fosters unity this week.

Day 149: Serving One Another

- **Scripture:** "Serve one another humbly in love." — Galatians 5:13
- **Reflection:** Serving others is a cornerstone of intentional community.
- **Application:** Identify a need within the community and volunteer to help.

Day 150: Building Trust

- **Scripture:** "As iron sharpens iron, so one person sharpens another." — Proverbs 27:17
- **Reflection:** Trust is built through

honest relationships.

- **Application:** Share a personal story with someone in the group to build trust.

Day 151: The Importance of Communication

- **Scripture:** "Do not let any unwholesome talk come out of your mouths, but only what is helpful for building others up." — Ephesians 4:29
- **Reflection:** Effective communication strengthens community ties.
- **Application:** Practice active listening in your next conversation.

Day 152: Encouragement in Community

- **Scripture:** "And let us consider how we may spur one another on toward love and good deeds." — Hebrews 10:24-25
- **Reflection:** Encouragement fuels motivation.
- **Application:** Write an encouraging

note to a community member.

Day 153: Embracing Diversity

- **Scripture:** "After this I looked, and there before me was a great multitude that no one could count, from every nation, tribe, people and language." — Revelation 7:9
- **Reflection:** Diversity enriches our community experience.
- **Application:** Share a meal or tradition from your culture with the group.

Days 154–160

Weekly Prayer:

Help me to know myself deeply and truthfully.

Day 154: The Role of Forgiveness

- **Scripture:** "Bear with each other and forgive one another if any of you has a grievance against someone." — Colossians 3:13
- **Reflection:** Forgiveness is essential for healthy relationships.
- **Application:** Reflect on someone you need to forgive and take a step toward reconciliation.

Day 155: The Gift of Hospitality

- **Scripture:** - "Offer hospitality to one another without grumbling." — 1 Peter 4:9
- **Reflection:** Hospitality creates a welcoming environment.
- **Application:** Invite someone from the community over for a meal or coffee.

Day 156: Prayer as a Community

- **Scripture:** "For where two or three gather in my name, there am I with them." – Matthew 18:20
- **Reflection:** Prayer strengthens our connection with God and each other.
- **Application:** Organize a prayer meeting or prayer partner system.

Day 157: Sharing Resources

- **Scripture:** "At the present time your plenty will supply what they need…" — 2 Corinthians 8:14

- **Reflection:** Sharing resources fosters support and equity.
- **Application:** Identify a resource you can share with someone in need.

Day 158: The Impact of Accountability

- **Scripture:** “Wounds from a friend can be trusted, but an enemy multiplies kisses.” — Proverbs 27:6
- **Reflection:** Accountability helps us grow.
- **Application:** Find an accountability partner within the community.

Day 159: The Importance of Gratitude

- **Scripture:** “Give thanks in all circumstances; for this is God’s will for you in Christ Jesus.” — 1 Thessalonians 5:18
- **Reflection:** Gratitude enhances our perspective.

- **Application:** Share three things you are grateful for in the community.

Day 160: The Power of Testimony

- **Scripture:** "They triumphed over him by the blood of the Lamb and by the word of their testimony." — Revelation 12:11
- **Reflection:** Sharing our stories strengthens faith.
- **Application:** Prepare to share your testimony in a group setting.

Days 161–167

Weekly Prayer:

Teach me to accept myself fully and unconditionally.

Day 161: Cultivating Patience

- **Scripture:** "Be completely humble and gentle; be patient, bearing with one another in love." — Ephesians 4:2
- **Reflection:** Patience is vital in relationships.
- **Application:** Practice patience in a challenging interaction today.

Day 162: The Call to Love

- **Scripture:** - "A new command I give you: Love one another." – John 13:34
- **Reflection:** Love is the foundation of community.
- **Application:** Perform a random act of kindness for someone in the community.

Day 163: The Importance of Boundaries

- **Scripture:** "For each one should carry their own load." — Galatians 6:5
- **Reflection:** Healthy boundaries protect relationships.
- **Application:** Reflect on a boundary you need to establish in your life.

Day 164: The Role of Mentorship

- **Scripture:** "Let the wise hear and increase in learning, and the one who understands obtain guidance." — Proverbs 1:5

- **Reflection:** Mentorship fosters growth and wisdom.
- **Application:** Seek out a mentor or offer to mentor someone else.

Day 165: The Gift of Listening

- **Scripture:** "Everyone should be quick to listen, slow to speak and slow to become angry." —James 1:19
- **Reflection:** Listening fosters understanding.
- **Application:** Practice active listening in your next conversation.

Day 166: Spiritual Gifts in Community

- **Scripture:** "There are different kinds of gifts, but the same Spirit distributes them." — 1 Corinthians 12:4-7
- **Reflection:** Each member has unique gifts to contribute.
- **Application:** Identify your spiritual gifts and how you can use them in the

community.

Day 167: The Value of Commitment

- **Scripture:** "Two are better than one, because they have a good return for their labor." — Ecclesiastes 4:9
- **Reflection:** Commitment strengthens community.
- **Application:** Reflect on your commitment to the community and how you can deepen it.

Days 168–174

Weekly Prayer:

Send me the guidance I need on my spiritual path.

Day 168: The Importance of Celebration

- **Scripture:** "The Lord has done great things for us, and we are filled with joy." — Psalm 126:3
- **Reflection:** Celebrating together fosters joy and connection.
- **Application:** Plan a celebration for a recent achievement in the community.

Day 169: The Role of Hope

- **Scripture:** "May the God of hope fill you with all joy and peace as you trust in him." — Romans 15:13

- Reflection: Hope sustains us through challenges.

- **Application:** Share a hopeful message or scripture with someone who needs encouragement.

Day 170: Embracing Change

- **Scripture:** "See, I am doing a new thing! Now it springs up; do you not perceive it?" — Isaiah 43:19

- **Reflection:** Change can lead to growth and new opportunities.

- **Application:** Reflect on a recent change in your life and how it has shaped you.

Day 171: The Importance of Rest

- **Scripture:** "Come with me by yourselves to a quiet place and get some rest." — Mark 6:31

- **Reflection:** Rest is essential for our well-being.
- **Application:** Schedule a time for rest and reflection this week.

Day 172: The Power of Faith

- **Scripture:** "Now faith is confidence in what we hope for and assurance about what we do not see." — Hebrews 11:1
- **Reflection:** Faith unites us as a community.
- **Application:** Share a story of how faith has impacted your life.

Day 173: The Role of Creativity

- **Scripture:** "He has filled them with skills to do all kinds of work." — Exodus 35:35
- **Reflection:** Creativity enhances community life.
- **Application:** Organize a creative activity for the community to enjoy

together.

Day 174: The Importance of Authenticity

- **Scripture:** "We prove ourselves by our purity, our understanding, our patience, our kindness…" — 2 Corinthians 6:6
- **Reflection:** Authenticity builds trust and connection.
- **Application:** Share a personal struggle with a trusted community member.

Days 175–181

Weekly Prayer:

I surrender my worries and fears to you, trusting in your plan.

Day 175: The Value of Learning

- **Scripture:** "The heart of the discerning acquires knowledge, for the ears of the wise seek it out." — Proverbs 18:15
- **Reflection:** Continuous learning enriches our community.
- **Application:** Choose a book or resource to study as a group.

Day 176: The Gift of Time

- **Scripture:** "Be very careful, then, how you live—not as unwise but as wise, making the most of every opportunity." — Ephesians 5:15-16

- **Reflection:** Time is a valuable gift we share with one another.

- **Application:** Dedicate time to spend with someone from the community.

Day 177: The Power of Kindness

- **Scripture:** "Those who are kind benefit themselves, but the cruel bring ruin on themselves." — Proverbs 11:17

- **Reflection:** Kindness creates a positive atmosphere.

- **Application:** Perform an act of kindness for a stranger today.

Day 178: The Importance of Reflection

- **Scripture:** "Search me, God, and know

my heart; test me and know my anxious thoughts." — Psalm 139:23-24

- **Reflection:** Reflection leads to personal and communal growth.
- **Application:** Spend time in prayerful reflection about your role in the community.

Day 179: The Role of Hope

- Scripture: "For I know the plans I have for you, declares the Lord." Jeremiah 29:11
- Reflection: Hope shapes our future.
- Application: Share your hopes for the community with others.

Day 180: The Importance of Sharing

- **Scripture:** "It is more blessed to give than to receive." — Acts 20:35
- **Reflection:** Sharing fosters connection and generosity.
- **Application:** Organize a community

resource-sharing event.

Day 181: The Power of Vision

- **Scripture:** "Where there is no vision, the people perish." — Proverbs 29:18
- **Reflection:** A shared vision unites and motivates the community.
- **Application:** Collaborate with others to create a vision statement for your community.

DAYS 182–188

Weekly Prayer:

Help me reflect on my spiritual journey thus far.

Day 182: The Importance of Compassion

- **Scripture:** "Therefore, as God's chosen people, holy and dearly loved, clothe yourselves with compassion." — Colossians 3:12
- **Reflection:** Compassion enriches our relationships.
- **Application:** Reach out to someone who is struggling and offer support.

Day 183: The Role of Joy

- **Scripture:** "The joy of the Lord is your strength." — Nehemiah 8:10
- **Reflection:** Joy strengthens our community.
- **Application:** Plan a joyful gathering to celebrate your community.

Day 184: The Importance of Integrity

- **Scripture:** "Whoever walks in integrity walks securely." — Proverbs 10:9
- **Reflection:** Integrity builds trust within the community.
- **Application:** Reflect on a situation where you can demonstrate integrity.

Day 185: The Power of Laughter

- **Scripture:** "A cheerful heart is good medicine." — Proverbs 17:22
- **Reflection:** Laughter fosters connection

and joy.

- **Application:** Share a funny story or joke with the group.

Day 186: The Importance of Vision

- **Scripture:** “Write down the revelation and make it plain on tablets so that a herald may run with it.” — Habakkuk 2:2
- **Reflection:** Vision guides our actions.
- **Application:** Create a vision board for your community goals.

Day 187: The Role of Humility

- **Scripture:** "Do nothing out of selfish ambition or vain conceit. Rather, in humility value others above yourselves.” — Philippians 2:3
- **Reflection:** Humility fosters collaboration.
- **Application:** Practice humility in a conversation today.

Day 188: The Importance of Support

- **Scripture:** "If either of them falls down, one can help the other up." — Ecclesiastes 4:10
- **Reflection:** Support is vital in community life.
- **Application:** Offer your support to someone facing a challenge.

Days 189–195

Weekly Prayer:

I commit to this journey of spiritual growth.

Day 189: The Power of Prayer

- **Scripture:** "Rejoice always, pray continually, give thanks in all circumstances." — 1 Thessalonians 5:16–18
- **Reflection:** Prayer strengthens our connection to God and each other.
- **Application:** Set aside time to pray for the needs of your community.

Day 190: The Importance of Commitment

- **Scripture:** "Just as a body, though one, has many parts…" — 1 Corinthians 12:12

- **Reflection:** Commitment to the community strengthens our collective mission.

- **Application:** Reflect on your commitment to the community and how you can deepen it.

Day 191: The Role of Hope

- **Scripture:** "Not only so, but we also glory in our sufferings, because we know that suffering produces perseverance; perseverance, character; and character, hope." — Romans 5:3-4

- **Reflection:** Hope sustains us through difficulties.

- **Application:** Share a story of hope in the face of adversity.

Day 192: The Importance of Reflection

- **Scripture:** "Let us examine our ways and test them, and let us return to the Lord." — Lamentations 3:40
- **Reflection:** Reflection leads to growth and understanding.
- **Application:** Spend time journaling about your experiences in the community.

Day 193: The Power of Presence

- **Scripture:** "And surely I am with you always, to the very end of the age." — Matthew 28:20
- **Reflection:** Being present for one another is a gift.
- **Application:** Make an effort to be present for someone today, offering your time and attention.

Day 194: The Importance of Compassion

- **Scripture:** "But a Samaritan, as he traveled, came where the man was; and when he saw him, he took pity on him." — Luke 10:33-34

- **Reflection:** Compassion compels us to act.

- **Application:** Identify a need in your community and address it with compassion.

Day 195: The Role of Faith

- **Scripture:** "Now faith is confidence in what we hope for and assurance about what we do not see." — Hebrews 11:1

- **Reflection:** Faith unites us in purpose.

- **Application:** Share a faith-related goal with someone in the community.

DAYS 196–202

Weekly Prayer:

Teach me to embrace my imperfections and learn from them.

Day 196: The Importance of Kindness

- **Scripture:** "Be kind and compassionate to one another, forgiving each other, just as in Christ God forgave you." — Ephesians 4:32
- **Reflection:** Kindness fosters a positive atmosphere.
- **Application:** Perform a random act of kindness for someone today.

Day 197: The Power of Shared Experiences

- **Scripture:** "Two are better than one, because they have a good return for their labor." — Ecclesiastes 4:9
- **Reflection:** Shared experiences strengthen community bonds.
- **Application:** Organize a group outing or activity to create shared memories.

Day 198: The Role of Gratitude

- Scripture: "Let the peace of Christ rule in your hearts, since as members of one body you were called to peace. And be thankful." — Colossians 3:15
- **Reflection:** Gratitude enhances our relationships.
- **Application:** Share something you are grateful for in the community.

Day 199: The Importance of Empathy

- **Scripture:** "Rejoice with those who rejoice; mourn with those who mourn." — Romans 12:15

- **Reflection:** Empathy deepens our connections.

- **Application:** Reach out to someone who is experiencing a difficult time and offer support.

Day 200: The Role of Joy

- **Scripture:** - "The Lord has done great things for us, and we are filled with joy." — Psalm 126:3

- **Reflection:** Joy is a gift that strengthens community.

- **Application:** Plan a joyful gathering to celebrate your community.

Day 201: The Importance of Learning

- **Scripture:** "Let the wise hear and increase in learning, and the one who understands obtain guidance." — Proverbs 1:5
- **Reflection:** Continuous learning enriches our community.
- **Application:** Choose a topic to study as a group and discuss its relevance.

Day 202: The Power of Listening

- **Scripture:** "To answer before listening—that is folly and shame." — Proverbs 18:13
- **Reflection:** Listening fosters understanding and connection.
- **Application:** Practice active listening in your next conversation.

Days 203–209

Weekly Prayer:

Teach me to embrace my imperfections and learn from them.

Day 203: The Importance of Commitment

- **Scripture:** "For if the willingness is there, the gift is acceptable according to what one has, not according to what one does not have." — 2 Corinthians 8:12
- **Reflection:** Commitment to the community strengthens our collective mission.
- **Application:** Reflect on your

commitment to the community and how you can deepen it.

Day 204: The Role of Service

- **Scripture:** "For even the Son of Man did not come to be served, but to serve." — Mark 10:45
- **Reflection:** Service is a hallmark of community.
- **Application:** Identify a service opportunity in your community and participate.

Day 205: The Importance of Trust

- **Scripture:** "Trust in the Lord with all your heart and lean not on your own understanding." — Proverbs 3:5-6
- **Reflection:** Trust is foundational for healthy relationships.
- **Application:** Reflect on ways to build trust within the community.

Day 206: The Power of Hope

- **Scripture:** "May the God of hope fill you with all joy and peace as you trust in him." — Romans 15:13
- **Reflection:** Hope sustains us through challenges.
- **Application:** Share a hopeful message with someone who needs encouragement.

Day 207: The Importance of Reflection

- **Scripture:** "Search me, God, and know my heart; test me and know my anxious thoughts." — Psalm 139:23-24
- **Reflection:** Reflection leads to personal and communal growth.
- **Application:** Spend time in prayerful reflection about your role in the community.

Day 208: The Role of Compassion

- **Scripture:** "Dear children, let us not love with words or speech but with actions and in truth." — 1 John 3:18
- **Reflection:** Compassion compels us to act.
- **Application:** Identify a need in your community and address it with compassion.

Day 209: The Importance of Togetherness

- **Scripture:** "For where two or three gather in my name, there am I with them." — Matthew 18:20
- **Reflection:** Togetherness strengthens our bond with God and each other.
- **Application:** Organize a gathering for prayer or fellowship.

DAYS 210–219

Weekly Prayer:

Thank you for the blessings in my life; help me recognize them.

Day 210: The Power of Joy

- **Scripture:** "The joy of the Lord is your strength." — Nehemiah 8:10
- **Reflection:** Joy strengthens our community.
- **Application:** Plan a joyful gathering to celebrate your community.

Day 211: The Importance of Service

- **Scripture:** “Carry each other’s burdens, and in this way you will fulfill the law of Christ.” — Galatians 6:2
- **Reflection:** Service is a hallmark of community.
- **Application:** Identify a service opportunity in your community and participate.

Day 212: The Role of Faith

- **Scripture:** “Now faith is confidence in what we hope for and assurance about what we do not see.” — Hebrews 11:1
- **Reflection:** Faith unites us in purpose.
- **Application:** Share a faith-related goal with someone in the community.

Day 213: The Importance of Commitment

- **Scripture:** “For if the willingness is there, the gift is acceptable according to what one has, not according to what one does not have." — 2 Corinthians 8:12

- **Reflection:** Commitment to the community strengthens our collective mission.
- **Application:** Reflect on your commitment to the community and how you can deepen it.

Day 214: The Power of Presence

- **Scripture:** "And surely I am with you always, to the very end of the age." — Matthew 28:20
- **Reflection:** Being present for one another is a gift.
- **Application:** Make an effort to be present for someone today, offering your time and attention.

Day 215: The Role of Forgiveness

- **Scripture:** "For if you forgive other people when they sin against you, your heavenly Father will also forgive you." — Matthew 6:14

- **Reflection:** Forgiveness is essential for healthy relationships.
- **Application:** Reflect on someone you need to forgive and take a step toward reconciliation.

Day 216: The Importance of Gratitude

- **Scripture:** "Give thanks in all circumstances; for this is God's will for you in Christ Jesus." — 1 Thessalonians 5:18
- **Reflection:** Gratitude enhances our perspective.
- **Application:** Share three things you are grateful for in the community.

Day 217: The Power of Listening

- **Scripture:** "To answer before listening—that is folly and shame." — Proverbs 18:13
- **Reflection:** Listening fosters understanding and connection.

- **Application:** Practice active listening in your next conversation.

Day 218: The Importance of Learning

- **Scripture:** "Let the wise hear and increase in learning, and the one who understands obtain guidance." — Proverbs 1:5
- **Reflection:** Continuous learning enriches our community.
- **Application:** Choose a topic to study as a group and discuss its relevance.

Day 219: The Call to Action

- **Scripture:** "In the same way, faith by itself, if it is not accompanied by action, is dead." — James 2:17
- **Reflection:** Our faith should inspire action within the community.
- **Application:** Identify a specific action you can take this week to support the community.

NURTURING OTHERS

Days 220–226

Weekly Prayer:

Lord, help me to clarify my intention for this journey.

Day 220: The Call to Nurture

- **Scripture:** "Therefore encourage one another and build each other up." — 1 Thessalonians 5:11

- **Reflection:** Nurturing others starts with encouragement.

- **Application:** Write an encouraging note to someone today.

Day 221: The Power of Compassion

- **Scripture:** "Therefore, as God's chosen people, holy and dearly loved, clothe yourselves with compassion." — Colossians 3:12

- **Reflection:** Compassion is a vital aspect of nurturing.

- **Application:** Identify someone who needs compassion and reach out to them.

Day 222: Listening with Intent

- **Scripture:** "Everyone should be quick to listen, slow to speak and slow to become angry." — James 1:19

- **Reflection:** Active listening is a powerful way to nurture relationships.

- **Application:** Practice active listening in your next conversation.

Day 223: The Gift of Time

- **Scripture:** "Be very careful, then, how you live—not as unwise but as wise, making the most of every opportunity." — Ephesians 5:15-16

- **Reflection:** Time is a precious gift we can give to others.

- **Application:** Set aside dedicated time to spend with someone who needs your support.

Day 224: Acts of Kindness

- **Scripture:** "Those who are kind benefit themselves, but the cruel bring ruin on themselves." — Proverbs 11:17

- **Reflection:** Kindness creates a ripple effect of positivity.

- **Application:** Perform a random act of kindness today.

Day 225: The Importance of Forgiveness

- **Scripture:** "Be kind and compassionate to one another, forgiving each other, just as in Christ God forgave you." — Ephesians 4:32

- **Reflection:** Forgiveness is essential for nurturing relationships.
- **Application:** Reflect on someone you need to forgive and take a step toward reconciliation.

Day 226: Sharing Burdens

- **Scripture:** "Carry each other's burdens, and in this way you will fulfill the law of Christ." — Galatians 6:2
- **Reflection:** Supporting one another is a key aspect of nurturing.
- **Application:** Offer to help someone with a burden they are carrying.

Days 227–233

Weekly Prayer:

Help me to know myself deeply and truthfully.

Day 227: The Role of Patience

- **Scripture:** "Love is patient, love is kind." — 1 Corinthians 13:4
- **Reflection:** Patience is a vital component of nurturing.
- **Application:** Practice patience in a challenging situation today.

Day 228: Celebrating Others

- **Scripture:** "Rejoice with those who

rejoice; mourn with those who mourn." — Romans 12:15

- **Reflection:** Celebrating others strengthens community bonds.
- **Application:** Acknowledge someone's achievement or milestone today.

Day 229: The Power of Encouragement

- **Scripture:** "And let us consider how we may spur one another on toward love and good deeds." — Hebrews 10:24-25
- **Reflection:** Encouragement motivates and uplifts.
- **Application:** Send a message of encouragement to someone in your life.

Day 230: The Importance of Empathy

- **Scripture:** "Finally, all of you, be like-minded, be sympathetic, love one another, be compassionate and humble." — 1 Peter 3:8

- **Reflection:** Empathy fosters deeper connections.
- **Application:** Try to see a situation from someone else's perspective today.

Day 231: The Gift of Presence

- **Scripture:** "And surely I am with you always, to the very end of the age." — Matthew 28:20
- **Reflection:** Being present for others is a powerful form of nurturing.
- **Application:** Spend quality time with someone today without distractions.

Day 232: The Role of Prayer

- **Scripture:** "Do not be anxious about anything, but in every situation, by prayer and petition, with thanksgiving, present your requests to God." — Philippians 4:6-7
- **Reflection:** Prayer supports and nurtures our relationships.
- **Application:** Pray for someone in your

life who needs support.

Day 233: The Importance of Boundaries

- **Scripture:** "For each one should carry their own load." — Galatians 6:5
- **Reflection:** Healthy boundaries are necessary for nurturing relationships.
- **Application:** Reflect on a boundary you need to set to maintain healthy relationships.

Days 234–240

Weekly Prayer:

Teach me to accept myself fully and unconditionally.

Day 234: The Power of Gratitude

- **Scripture:** "Give thanks in all circumstances; for this is God's will for you in Christ Jesus." — 1 Thessalonians 5:18
- **Reflection:** Gratitude enhances our perspective and relationships.
- **Application:** Share three things you are grateful for about someone in your life.

Day 235: The Role of Mentorship

- **Scripture:** "As iron sharpens iron, so one person sharpens another." — Proverbs 27:17
- **Reflection:** Mentorship nurtures growth and development.
- **Application:** Seek out a mentor or offer to mentor someone.

Day 236: The Importance of Authenticity

- **Scripture:** "We prove ourselves by our purity, our understanding, our patience, our kindness…" — 2 Corinthians 6:6
- **Reflection:** Authenticity builds trust in relationships.
- **Application:** Share something personal with a trusted friend to deepen your connection.

Day 237: The Gift of Affirmation

- **Scripture:** "Anxiety weighs down the

heart, but a kind word cheers it up." — Proverbs 12:25

- **Reflection:** Affirmation can uplift and nurture those around us.
- **Application:** Compliment someone sincerely today.

Day 238: The Role of Service

- **Scripture:** "For even the Son of Man did not come to be served, but to serve." — Mark 10:45
- **Reflection:** Serving others is a powerful way to nurture.
- **Application:** Volunteer your time or skills to help someone in need.

Day 239: The Importance of Hope

- **Scripture:** "May the God of hope fill you with all joy and peace as you trust in him." — Romans 15:13
- **Reflection:** Hope nurtures our spirits and those around us.

- **Application:** Share a message of hope with someone who is feeling discouraged.

Day 240: The Power of Vulnerability

- **Scripture:** "My grace is sufficient for you, for my power is made perfect in weakness." — 2 Corinthians 12:9

- **Reflection:** Vulnerability fosters genuine connections.

- **Application:** Share a struggle you are facing with a trusted friend.

Days 241–247

Weekly Prayer:

Send me the guidance I need on my spiritual path.

Day 241: The Importance of Community

- **Scripture:** "And let us consider how we may spur one another on toward love and good deeds, not giving up meeting together." — Hebrews 10:24-25
- **Reflection:** Community nurtures and supports us.
- **Application:** Attend a community event or gathering this week.

Day 242: The Role of Joy

- **Scripture:** "The joy of the Lord is your strength." — Nehemiah 8:10
- **Reflection:** Joy is contagious and nurturing.
- **Application:** Share something that brings you joy with someone else.

Day 243: The Importance of Learning

- **Scripture:** "Let the wise hear and increase in learning, and the one who understands obtain guidance." — Proverbs 1:5
- **Reflection:** Learning together nurtures growth.
- **Application**: Choose a book or resource to study with someone.

Day 244: The Power of Faith

- **Scripture:** "Now faith is confidence in what we hope for and assurance about what we do not see." — Hebrews 11:1

- **Reflection:** Faith nurtures hope and perseverance.
- **Application:** Share your faith journey with someone who may benefit from it.

Day 245: The Importance of Reflection

- **Scripture:** "Let us examine our ways and test them, and let us return to the Lord." — Lamentations 3:40
- **Reflection:** Reflection leads to personal growth and nurturing.
- **Application:** Spend time journaling about your experiences in nurturing others.

Day 246: The Role of Kindness

- **Scripture:** "Whoever pursues righteousness and love finds life, prosperity, and honor." — Proverbs 21:21
- **Reflection:** Kindness is a key

component of nurturing.

- **Application:** Perform a random act of kindness for a stranger today.

Day 247: The Importance of Support

- **Scripture:** "If either of them falls down, one can help the other up." — Ecclesiastes 4:10
- **Reflection:** Support is vital in nurturing relationships.
- **Application:** Offer to help someone who is struggling today.

Days 248–254

Weekly Prayer:

I surrender my worries and fears to you, trusting in your plan.

Day 248: The Power of Healing

- **Scripture:** "Therefore confess your sins to each other and pray for each other so that you may be healed." —James 5:16
- **Reflection:** Healing occurs in community.
- **Application:** Share a burden with someone and pray together.

Day 249: The Importance of Trust

- **Scripture:** "Trust in the Lord with all your heart and lean not on your own understanding." — Proverbs 3:5
- **Reflection:** Trust is foundational in nurturing relationships.
- **Application:** Reflect on ways to build trust within your relationships.

Day 250: The Role of Hope

- **Scripture:** "For I know the plans I have for you, declares the Lord." — Jeremiah 29:11
- **Reflection:** Hope sustains us through challenges.
- **Application:** Share a hopeful message with someone who needs encouragement.

Day 251: The Importance of Communication

- **Scripture:** "Do not let any

unwholesome talk come out of your mouths, but only what is helpful for building others up." — Ephesians 4:29

- **Reflection:** Effective communication nurtures relationships.
- **Application:** Practice positive communication in your conversations today.

Day 252: The Power of Faithfulness

Scripture: "Let love and faithfulness never leave you; bind them around your neck, write them on the tablet of your heart." — Proverbs 3:3

Reflection: Faithfulness nurtures trust and stability.

Application: Reflect on how you can be more faithful in your relationships.

Day 253: The Importance of Joy

- **Scripture:** "The Lord has done great things for us, and we are filled with joy." — Psalm 126:3
- **Reflection:** Joy strengthens our community.

- **Application:** Plan a joyful gathering to celebrate your community.

Day 254: The Role of Humility

- **Scripture:** "Do nothing out of selfish ambition or vain conceit. Rather, in humility value others above yourselves." — Philippians 2:3
- **Reflection:** Humility fosters understanding and connection.
- **Application:** Practice humility in a conversation today.

Days 255–261

Weekly Prayer:

Help me reflect on my spiritual journey thus far.

Day 255: The Importance of Reflection

- **Scripture:** "Search me, God, and know my heart; test me and know my anxious thoughts." — Psalm 139:23-24
- **Reflection:** Reflection leads to personal and communal growth.
- **Application:** Spend time journaling about your experiences in nurturing others.

Day 256: The Power of Connection

Scripture: "For where two or three gather in my name, there am I with them." — Matthew 18:20

Reflection: Connection enhances our relationships.

Application: Organize a gathering for prayer or fellowship.

Day 257: The Importance of Empathy

Scripture: "Rejoice with those who rejoice; mourn with those who mourn." — Romans 12:15

Reflection: Empathy deepens our connections.

Application: Reach out to someone who is experiencing a difficult time and offer support.

Day 258: The Role of Service

Scripture: "Serve one another humbly in love." — Galatians 5:13

Reflection: Serving others is a powerful way to nurture.

Application: Identify a service opportunity in your community and participate.

Day 259: The Importance of Trust

Scripture: "A gossip betrays a confidence, but a trustworthy person keeps a secret." — Proverbs 11:13

Reflection: Trust is foundational for healthy relationships.

Application: Reflect on ways to build trust within the community.

Day 260: The Power of Encouragement

Scripture: "Therefore encourage one another and build each other up." — 1 Thessalonians 5:11

Reflection: Encouragement is vital for nurturing others.

Application: Send an encouraging message to someone today.

Day 261: The Importance of Kindness

Scripture: "Whoever is kind to the poor lends to the Lord, and he will reward them for what they have done." — Proverbs 19:17

Reflection: Kindness is a reflection of God's love.

Application: Find a way to be kind to someone in need today.

Days 262–268

Weekly Prayer:

I commit to this journey of spiritual growth.

Day 262: The Role of Joy

- **Scripture:** "Weeping may stay for the night, but rejoicing comes in the morning." — Psalm 30:5

- **Reflection:** Joy is a powerful force for healing and nurturing.

- **Application:** Share something that brings you joy with someone else.

Day 263: The Importance of Community

- **Scripture:** "And let us consider how we may spur one another on toward love and good deeds." — Hebrews 10:24-25
- **Reflection:** Community nurtures and supports us.
- **Application:** Attend a community event or gathering this week.

Day 264: The Power of Presence

- **Scripture:** "Who comforts us in all our troubles, so that we can comfort those in any trouble." — 2 Corinthians 1:4
- **Reflection:** Being present for others is a powerful form of nurturing.
- **Application:** Make an effort to be present for someone today, offering your time and attention.

Day 265: The Importance of Reflection

- **Scripture:** "Let us examine our ways and test them, and let us return to the Lord." — Lamentations 3:40

- **Reflection:** Reflection leads to personal growth and nurturing.

- **Application:** Spend time journaling about your experiences in nurturing others.

Day 266: The Role of Hope

- **Scripture:** "Be joyful in hope, patient in affliction, faithful in prayer." — Romans 12:12

- **Reflection:** Hope nurtures our spirits and those around us.

- **Application:** Share a message of hope with someone who is feeling discouraged.

Day 267: The Importance of Learning

- **Scripture:** "The heart of the discerning acquires knowledge, for the ears of the wise seek it out." — Proverbs 18:15
- **Reflection:** Continuous learning enriches our community.
- **Application:** Choose a topic to study as a group and discuss its relevance.

Day 268: The Power of Faith

- **Scripture:** "Now faith is confidence in what we hope for and assurance about what we do not see." — Hebrews 11:1
- **Reflection:** Faith unites us in purpose.
- **Application:** Share your faith journey with someone who may benefit from it.

Days 269–275

Weekly Prayer:

Teach me to embrace my imperfections and learn from them.

Day 269: The Importance of Kindness

- **Scripture:** “Be kind and compassionate to one another, forgiving each other, just as in Christ God forgave you.” — Ephesians 4:32
- **Reflection:** Kindness fosters a positive atmosphere.
- **Application:** Perform a random act of kindness for someone today.

Day 270: The Role of Service

- **Scripture:** "For even the Son of Man did not come to be served, but to serve." — Mark 10:45

- **Reflection:** Serving others is a hallmark of nurturing.

- **Application:** Volunteer your time or skills to help someone in need.

Day 271: The Importance of Connection

- **Scripture:** "Let your light shine before others, that they may see your good deeds and glorify your Father in heaven." — Matthew 5:16

- **Reflection:** Connection enhances our relationships.

- **Application:** Share a positive experience you've had in the community.

Day 272: The Power of Healing

- **Scripture:** "Therefore confess your sins

to each other and pray for each other so that you may be healed." — James 5:16

- **Reflection:** Healing occurs in community.
- **Application:** Share a burden with someone and pray together.

Day 273: The Importance of Trust

- **Scripture:** "Trust in the Lord with all your heart and lean not on your own understanding." — Proverbs 3:5-6
- **Reflection:** Trust is foundational for healthy relationships.
- **Application:** Reflect on ways to build trust within your relationships.

Day 274: The Role of Joy

- **Scripture:** "The joy of the Lord is your strength." — Nehemiah 8:10
- **Reflection:** Joy strengthens our community.
- **Application:** Plan a joyful gathering to

celebrate your community.

Day 275: The Importance of Support

- **Scripture:** "If either of them falls down, one can help the other up." — Ecclesiastes 4:10
- **Reflection:** Support is vital in nurturing relationships.
- **Application:** Offer to help someone who is struggling today.

Days 276–282

Weekly Prayer:

Teach me to embrace my imperfections and learn from them.

Day 276: The Power of Presence

- **Scripture:** "Who comforts us in all our troubles, so that we can comfort those in any trouble." — 2 Corinthians 1:4
- **Reflection:** Being present for others is a powerful form of nurturing.
- **Application:** Make an effort to be present for someone today, offering your time and attention.

Day 277: The Importance of Empathy

- **Scripture:** "Rejoice with those who rejoice; mourn with those who mourn." — Romans 12:15
- **Reflection:** Empathy deepens our connections.
- **Application:** Reach out to someone who is experiencing a difficult time and offer support.

Day 278: The Role of Kindness

- **Scripture:** "Whoever pursues righteousness and love finds life, prosperity, and honor." — Proverbs 21:21
- **Reflection:** Kindness is a reflection of God's love.
- **Application:** Find a way to be kind to someone in need today.

Day 279: The Importance of Community

- **Scripture:** "And let us consider how we may spur one another on toward love and good deeds." — Hebrews 10:24-25

- **Reflection:** Community nurtures and supports us.

- **Application:** Attend a community event or gathering this week.

Day 280: The Power of Faithfulness

- **Scripture:** "Let love and faithfulness never leave you; bind them around your neck, write them on the tablet of your heart." — Proverbs 3:3

- **Reflection:** Faithfulness nurtures trust and stability.

- **Application:** Reflect on how you can be more faithful in your relationships.

Day 281: The Importance of Reflection

- **Scripture:** "Let us examine our ways and test them, and let us return to the Lord." — Lamentations 3:40
- **Reflection:** Reflection leads to personal growth and nurturing.
- **Application:** Spend time journaling about your experiences in nurturing others.

Day 282: The Role of Service

- **Scripture:** "Serve one another humbly in love." — Galatians 5:13
- **Reflection:** Serving others is a powerful way to nurture.
- **Application:** Identify a service opportunity in your community and participate.

Days 283–292

Weekly Prayer:

Thank you for the blessings in my life; help me recognize them.

Day 283: The Importance of Trust

- **Scripture:** "A gossip betrays a confidence, but a trustworthy person keeps a secret." — Proverbs 11:13
- **Reflection:** Trust is foundational for healthy relationships.
- **Application:** Reflect on ways to build trust within the community.

Day 284: The Power of Encouragement

- **Scripture:** "Therefore encourage one another and build each other up." — 1 Thessalonians 5:11
- **Reflection:** Encouragement is vital for nurturing others.
- **Application:** Send an encouraging message to someone today.

Day 285: The Importance of Kindness

- **Scripture:** "Whoever is kind to the poor lends to the Lord, and he will reward them for what they have done." — Proverbs 19:17
- **Reflection:** Kindness is a reflection of God's love.
- **Application:** Find a way to be kind to someone in need today.

Day 286: The Role of Joy

- **Scripture:** "Weeping may stay for the night, but rejoicing comes in the morning." – Psalm 30:5
- **Reflection:** Joy is a powerful force for healing and nurturing.
- **Application:** Share something that brings you joy with someone else.

Day 287: The Importance of Community

- **Scripture:** "And let us consider how we may spur one another on toward love and good deeds." – Hebrews 10:24-25
- **Reflection:** Community nurtures and supports us.
- **Application:** Attend a community event or gathering this week.

Day 288: The Power of Presence

- **Scripture:** "Who comforts us in all our troubles, so that we can comfort those in any trouble." — 2 Corinthians 1:4

- **Reflection:** Being present for others is a powerful form of nurturing.

- **Application:** Make an effort to be present for someone today, offering your time and attention.

Day 289: The Importance of Empathy

- **Scripture:** "Rejoice with those who rejoice; mourn with those who mourn." — Romans 12:15

- **Reflection:** Empathy deepens our connections.

- **Application:** Reach out to someone who is experiencing a difficult time and offer support.

Day 290: The Role of Kindness

- **Scripture:** "Whoever pursues righteousness and love finds life, prosperity, and honor." — Proverbs 21:21

- **Reflection:** Kindness is a reflection of God's love.
- **Application:** Find a way to be kind to someone in need today.

Day 291: The Importance of Reflection

- **Scripture:** "Search me, God, and know my heart; test me and know my anxious thoughts." — Psalm 139:23-24
- **Reflection:** Reflection leads to personal and communal growth.
- **Application:** Spend time journaling about your experiences in nurturing others.

Day 292: The Call to Action

- **Scripture:** "In the same way, faith by itself, if it is not accompanied by action, is dead." — James 2:17
- **Reflection:** Our faith should inspire action in nurturing others.
- **Application:** Identify a specific action

you can take this week to nurture someone in your life.

EMOTIONAL RESILIENCE

Days 293–300

Weekly Prayer:

Lord, help me to clarify my intention for this journey.

Day 293: The Foundation of Resilience

- **Scripture:** "Consider it pure joy, my brothers and sisters, whenever you face trials of many kinds…" —James 1:2-4
- **Reflection:** Trials build resilience and character.
- **Application**: Reflect on a past challenge and how it has strengthened you.

Day 294: The Power of Faith

- **Scripture:** "Now faith is confidence in what we hope for and assurance about what we do not see." — Hebrews 11:1

- **Reflection:** Faith provides a foundation for emotional resilience.

- **Application:** Write down what you are hopeful for in your life.

Day 295: Embracing Change

- **Scripture:** "See, I am doing a new thing! Now it springs up; do you not perceive it?" — Isaiah 43:19

- **Reflection:** Change can lead to growth and new opportunities.

- **Application:** Identify a change you are currently facing and how you can embrace it.

Day 296: The Importance of Self-Care

- **Scripture:** "Do you not know that your

bodies are temples of the Holy Spirit?" — 1 Corinthians 6:19-20

- **Reflection:** Caring for yourself is essential for resilience.
- **Application:** Plan a self-care activity for today.

Day 297: The Role of Gratitude

- **Scripture:** "Give thanks in all circumstances; for this is God's will for you in Christ Jesus." — 1 Thessalonians 5:18
- **Reflection:** Gratitude shifts our focus and strengthens resilience.
- **Application:** Write down three things you are grateful for today.

Day 298: The Power of Community

- **Scripture:** "Two are better than one, because they have a good return for their labor." — Ecclesiastes 4:9-10
- **Reflection:** Community supports emotional resilience.

- **Application:** Reach out to a friend or family member for support today.

Day 299: The Importance of Forgiveness

- **Scripture:** "Be kind and compassionate to one another, forgiving each other, just as in Christ God forgave you." — Ephesians 4:32

- **Reflection:** Forgiveness frees us from emotional burdens.

- **Application:** Reflect on someone you need to forgive and take a step towards that.

Day 300: The Role of Hope

- **Scripture:** "May the God of hope fill you with all joy and peace as you trust in him." — Romans 15:13

- **Reflection:** Hope sustains us through difficult times.

- **Application:** Share a message of hope with someone who needs encouragement.

Days 301–307

Weekly Prayer:

Help me to know myself deeply and truthfully.

Day 301: The Importance of Boundaries

- **Scripture:** "For each will have to bear his own load." — Galatians 6:5
- **Reflection:** Healthy boundaries protect our emotional well-being.
- **Application:** Identify a boundary you need to set in your life.

Day 302: The Power of Joy

- **Scripture:** "The joy of the Lord is your strength." — Nehemiah 8:10
- **Reflection:** Joy strengthens our emotional resilience.
- **Application:** Do something today that brings you joy.

Day 303: The Importance of Mindfulness

- **Scripture:** "Do not be anxious about anything, but in every situation, by prayer and petition…" — Philippians 4:6-7
- **Reflection:** Mindfulness helps us manage anxiety.
- **Application:** Practice mindfulness for 10 minutes today.

Day 304: The Role of Patience

- **Scripture:** "Be joyful in hope, patient in affliction, faithful in prayer." — Romans

12:12

- **Reflection:** Patience is essential for emotional growth.
- **Application:** Reflect on a situation where you need to practice patience.

Day 305: The Power of Positive Thinking

- **Scripture:** "Finally, brothers and sisters, whatever is true, whatever is noble, whatever is right…" — Philippians 4:8
- **Reflection:** Positive thinking fosters resilience.
- **Application:** Write down three positive affirmations about yourself.

Day 306: The Importance of Emotional Awareness

- **Scripture:** "Search me, God, and know my heart; test me and know my anxious thoughts." — Psalm 139:23-24
- **Reflection:** Self-awareness is the first step to emotional resilience.

- **Application:** Journal about your emotions today. What are you feeling?

Day 307: The Role of Self-Compassion

- **Scripture:** "The steadfast love of the Lord never ceases; his mercies never come to an end." — Lamentations 3:22-23
- **Reflection:** Being kind to ourselves is crucial for resilience.
- **Application:** Treat yourself with the same kindness you would offer a friend.

Days 308–314

Weekly Prayer:

Teach me to accept myself fully and unconditionally.

Day 308: The Importance of Prayer

- **Scripture:** "Cast all your anxiety on him because he cares for you." — 1 Peter 5:7
- **Reflection:** Prayer is a source of strength and comfort.
- **Application:** Spend time in prayer today, bringing your worries to God.

Day 309: The Power of Resilience

- **Scripture:** "My grace is sufficient for you, for my power is made perfect in weakness." — 2 Corinthians 12:9

- **Reflection:** Resilience comes from recognizing our strengths in weakness.

- **Application:** Reflect on a time when you overcame a challenge.

Day 310: The Importance of Perspective

- **Scripture:** "And we know that in all things God works for the good of those who love him." — Romans 8:28

- **Reflection:** A positive perspective can change our emotional response.

- **Application:** Try to find the silver lining in a current challenge.

Day 311: The Role of Acceptance

- **Scripture:** "I have learned to be content whatever the circumstances." —

Philippians 4:11-12

- **Reflection:** Acceptance can lead to peace and resilience.
- **Application:** Reflect on something you need to accept in your life.

Day 312: The Power of Vulnerability

- **Scripture:** "For when I am weak, then I am strong." — 2 Corinthians 12:10
- **Reflection:** Vulnerability can be a source of strength.
- **Application:** Share a vulnerable moment with someone you trust.

Day 313: The Importance of Reflection

- **Scripture:** "Let us examine our ways and test them, and let us return to the Lord." — Lamentations 3:40
- **Reflection:** Reflection helps us grow and learn from our experiences.
- **Application:** Spend time journaling

about your recent experiences.

Day 314: The Role of Service

- **Scripture:** "For even the Son of Man did not come to be served, but to serve." — Mark 10:45
- **Reflection:** Serving others strengthens our emotional resilience.
- **Application:** Volunteer your time or skills to help someone in need.

Days 315–321

Weekly Prayer:

Send me the guidance I need on my spiritual path.

Day 315: The Importance of Trust

- **Scripture:** "Trust in the Lord with all your heart and lean not on your own understanding." — Proverbs 3:5-6
- **Reflection:** Trusting God enhances our resilience.
- **Application:** Reflect on an area where you need to trust God more.

Day 316: The Power of Laughter

- **Scripture:** "A cheerful heart is good medicine." — Proverbs 17:22

- **Reflection:** Laughter can lighten our burdens.

- **Application:** Watch a funny movie or share jokes with friends today.

Day 317: The Importance of Routine

- **Scripture:** "But everything should be done in a fitting and orderly way." — 1 Corinthians 14:40

- **Reflection:** Routines provide stability and support resilience.

- **Application:** Establish a daily routine that nurtures your emotional health.

Day 318: The Role of Hope

- **Scripture:** "For I know the plans I have for you, declares the Lord." — Jeremiah 29:11

- **Reflection:** Hope gives us a future and a

purpose.

- **Application:** Write down your hopes and dreams for the future.

Day 319: The Importance of Boundaries

- **Scripture:** "All you need to say is simply 'Yes' or 'No'; anything beyond this comes from the evil one." — Matthew 5:37
- **Reflection:** Setting boundaries protects our emotional health.
- **Application:** Identify a boundary you need to establish in your life.

Day 320: The Power of Affirmation

- **Scripture:** "The tongue has the power of life and death." — Proverbs 18:21
- **Reflection:** Our words can uplift or tear down.
- **Application:** Affirm someone today with kind words.

Day 321: The Importance of Learning

- **Scripture:** “Let the wise hear and increase in learning, and the one who understands obtain guidance.” — Proverbs 1:5
- **Reflection:** Learning from experiences enhances resilience.
- **Application:** Choose a lesson you’ve learned from a recent challenge.

Days 322–328

Weekly Prayer:

I surrender my worries and fears to you, trusting in your plan.

Day 322: The Role of Empathy

- **Scripture:** "Rejoice with those who rejoice; mourn with those who mourn." — Romans 12:15
- **Reflection:** Empathy strengthens our connections and resilience.
- **Application:** Reach out to someone who is struggling and offer support.

Day 323: The Importance of Balance

- **Scripture:** "There is a time for everything, and a season for every activity under the heavens." — Ecclesiastes 3:1
- **Reflection:** Balance in life promotes emotional health.
- **Application:** Assess areas of your life that need more balance.

Day 324: The Power of Self-Reflection

- **Scripture:** "I praise you because I am fearfully and wonderfully made." — Psalm 139:14
- **Reflection:** Self-reflection helps us understand our strengths and weaknesses.
- **Application:** Reflect on your unique qualities and strengths.

Day 325: The Importance of Hope

- **Scripture:** "Not only so, but we also glory in our sufferings, because we know that suffering produces perseverance." — Romans 5:3-4

- **Reflection:** Hope helps us endure difficult times.

- **Application:** Share a story of hope with someone who needs encouragement.

Day 326: The Role of Faith

- **Scripture:** "If you have faith as small as a mustard seed…" — Matthew 17:20

- **Reflection:** Even a little faith can lead to great resilience.

- **Application:** Identify a small step of faith you can take today.

Day 327: The Importance of Community

- **Scripture:** "Therefore encourage one another and build each other up." — 1

Thessalonians 5:11

- **Reflection:** Community provides support and strength.
- **Application:** Attend a community event or gathering this week.

Day 328: The Power of Acceptance

- **Scripture:** "I have learned to be content whatever the circumstances." — Philippians 4:11
- **Reflection:** Acceptance fosters peace and resilience.
- **Application:** Reflect on something you need to accept in your life.

Days 329–335

Weekly Prayer:

Help me reflect on my spiritual journey thus far.

Day 329: The Role of Vulnerability

- **Scripture:** "My grace is sufficient for you, for my power is made perfect in weakness." — 2 Corinthians 12:9
- **Reflection:** Vulnerability can lead to strength.
- **Application:** Share a vulnerable moment with someone you trust.

Day 330: The Importance of Reflection

- **Scripture:** "Let us examine our ways and test them, and let us return to the Lord." — Lamentations 3:40

- **Reflection:** Reflection leads to personal growth.

- **Application:** Spend time journaling about your recent experiences.

Day 331: The Power of Service

- **Scripture:** "Serve one another humbly in love." — Galatians 5:13

- **Reflection:** Serving others strengthens our emotional resilience.

- **Application:** Volunteer your time or skills to help someone in need.

Day 332: The Importance of Trust

- **Scripture:** "A gossip betrays a confidence, but a trustworthy person keeps a secret." — Proverbs 11:13

- **Reflection:** Trust is foundational for healthy relationships.
- **Application:** Reflect on ways to build trust within your relationships.

Day 333: The Role of Joy

- **Scripture:** "Weeping may stay for the night, but rejoicing comes in the morning." — Psalm 30:5
- **Reflection:** Joy is a powerful force for healing and resilience.
- **Application:** Share something that brings you joy with someone else.

Day 334: The Importance of Community

- **Scripture:** "And let us consider how we may spur one another on toward love and good deeds." — Hebrews 10:24-25
- **Reflection:** Community nurtures and supports us.
- **Application:** Attend a community event or gathering this week.

Day 335: The Power of Presence

- **Scripture:** "Who comforts us in all our troubles, so that we can comfort those in any trouble." — 2 Corinthians 1:4
- **Reflection:** Being present for others is a powerful form of nurturing.
- **Application:** Make an effort to be present for someone today.

Days 336–342

Weekly Prayer:

I commit to this journey of spiritual growth.

Day 336: The Importance of Empathy

- **Scripture**: "Rejoice with those who rejoice; mourn with those who mourn." — Romans 12:15
- **Reflection:** Empathy deepens our connections.
- **Application:** Reach out to someone who is experiencing a difficult time and offer support.

Day 337: The Role of Kindness

- **Scripture:** "Whoever pursues righteousness and love finds life, prosperity, and honor." — Proverbs 21:21

- **Reflection:** Kindness is a reflection of God's love.

- **Application:** Find a way to be kind to someone in need today.

Day 338: The Importance of Reflection

- **Scripture:** "Search me, God, and know my heart; test me and know my anxious thoughts." — Psalm 139:23-24

- **Reflection:** Reflection leads to personal and communal growth.

- **Application:** Spend time journaling about your experiences in nurturing others.

Day 339: The Role of Hope

- **Scripture:** "For I know the plans I have for you, declares the Lord." — Jeremiah 29:11
- **Reflection:** Hope gives us a future and a purpose.
- **Application:** Write down your hopes and dreams for the future.

Day 340: The Importance of Boundaries

- **Scripture:** "All you need to say is simply 'Yes' or 'No'; anything beyond this comes from the evil one." — Matthew 5:37
- **Reflection:** Setting boundaries protects our emotional health.
- **Application:** Identify a boundary you need to establish in your life.

Day 341: The Power of Affirmation

- **Scripture:** "The tongue has the power of

life and death." — Proverbs 18:21

- **Reflection:** Our words can uplift or tear down.
- **Application:** Affirm someone today with kind words.

Day 342: The Importance of Learning

Scripture: "Let the wise hear and increase in learning, and the one who understands obtain guidance." — Proverbs 1:5

Reflection: Continuous learning enriches our community.

Application: Choose a topic to study as a group and discuss its relevance.

DAYS 343–349

Weekly Prayer:

Teach me to embrace my imperfections and learn from them.

Day 343: The Power of Faith

- **Scripture:** "If you have faith as small as a mustard seed…" — Matthew 17:20
- **Reflection:** Even a little faith can lead to great resilience.
- **Application:** Identify a small step of faith you can take today.

Day 344: The Importance of Routine

- **Scripture:** "But everything should be done in a fitting and orderly way." — 1 Corinthians 14:40
- **Reflection:** Routines provide stability and support resilience.
- **Application:** Establish a daily routine that nurtures your emotional health.

Day 345: The Role of Empathy

- **Scripture:** "Rejoice with those who rejoice; mourn with those who mourn." — Romans 12:15
- **Reflection:** Empathy deepens our connections.
- **Application:** Reach out to someone who is experiencing a difficult time and offer support.

Day 346: The Importance of Trust

- **Scripture:** "Trust in the Lord with all your heart and lean not on your own understanding." — Proverbs 3:5-6

- **Reflection:** Trusting God enhances our resilience.
- **Application:** Reflect on an area where you need to trust God more.

Day 347: The Power of Laughter

- **Scripture:** "A cheerful heart is good medicine." — Proverbs 17:22
- **Reflection:** Laughter can lighten our burdens.
- **Application:** Watch a funny movie or share jokes with friends today.

Day 348: The Importance of Balance

- **Scripture:** "There is a time for everything, and a season for every activity under the heavens." — Ecclesiastes 3:1
- **Reflection:** Balance in life promotes emotional health.
- **Application:** Assess areas of your life

that need more balance.

Day 349: The Role of Self-Reflection

- **Scripture:** "I praise you because I am fearfully and wonderfully made." — Psalm 139:14
- **Reflection:** Self-reflection helps us understand our strengths and weaknesses.
- **Application:** Reflect on your unique qualities and strengths.

Days 350–356

Weekly Prayer:

Teach me to embrace my imperfections and learn from them.

Day 350: The Importance of Hope

- **Scripture:** "Not only so, but we also glory in our sufferings, because we know that suffering produces perseverance." — Romans 5:3–4
- **Reflection:** Hope helps us endure difficult times.
- **Application:** Share a story of hope with someone who needs encouragement.

Day 351: The Role of Faith

- **Scripture:** "Now faith is confidence in what we hope for and assurance about what we do not see." — Hebrews 11:1

- **Reflection:** Faith provides a foundation for emotional resilience.

- **Application:** Write down what you are hopeful for in your life.

Day 352: The Importance of Self-Care

- **Scripture:** "Do you not know that your bodies are temples of the Holy Spirit?" — 1 Corinthians 6:19-20

- **Reflection:** Caring for yourself is essential for resilience.

- **Application:** Plan a self-care activity for today.

Day 353: The Power of Perspective

- **Scripture:** "And we know that in all things God works for the good of those who love him." — Romans 8:28

- **Reflection:** A positive perspective can change our emotional response.
- **Application:** Try to find the silver lining in a current challenge.

Day 354: The Importance of Mindfulness

- **Scripture:** "Do not be anxious about anything, but in every situation, by prayer and petition…" — Philippians 4:6-7
- **Reflection:** Mindfulness helps us manage anxiety.
- **Application:** Practice mindfulness for 10 minutes today.

Day 355: The Role of Self-Compassion

- **Scripture:** "The steadfast love of the Lord never ceases; his mercies never come to an end." — Lamentations 3:22-23

- **Reflection:** Being kind to ourselves is crucial for resilience.
- **Application:** Treat yourself with the same kindness you would offer a friend.

Day 356: The Importance of Prayer

- **Scripture:** "Cast all your anxiety on him because he cares for you." — 1 Peter 5:7
- **Reflection:** Prayer is a source of strength and comfort.
- **Application:** Spend time in prayer today, bringing your worries to God.

DAYS 357–365

Weekly Prayer:

Thank you for the blessings in my life; help me recognize them.

Day 357: The Power of Resilience

- **Scripture:** "My grace is sufficient for you, for my power is made perfect in weakness." — 2 Corinthians 12:9
- **Reflection:** Resilience comes from recognizing our strengths in weakness.
- **Application:** Reflect on a time when you overcame a challenge.

Day 358: The Importance of Reflection

- **Scripture:** "Let us examine our ways and test them, and let us return to the Lord." — Lamentations 3:40

- **Reflection:** Reflection leads to personal growth.

- **Application:** Spend time journaling about your recent experiences.

Day 359: The Role of Kindness

- **Scripture:** "Whoever pursues righteousness and love finds life, prosperity, and honor." — Proverbs 21:21

- **Reflection:** Kindness is a reflection of God's love.

- **Application:** Find a way to be kind to someone in need today.

Day 360: The Importance of Community

- **Scripture:** "And let us consider how we may spur one another on toward love and good deeds." — Hebrews 10:24-25
- **Reflection:** Community nurtures and supports us.
- **Application:** Attend a community event or gathering this week.

Day 361: The Power of Presence

- **Scripture:** "Who comforts us in all our troubles, so that we can comfort those in any trouble." — 2 Corinthians 1:4
- **Reflection:** Being present for others is a powerful form of nurturing.
- **Application:** Make an effort to be present for someone today.

Day 362: The Importance of Empathy

- **Scripture:** "Rejoice with those who

rejoice; mourn with those who mourn." — Romans 12:15

- **Reflection:** Empathy deepens our connections.
- **Application:** Reach out to someone who is experiencing a difficult time and offer support.

Day 363: The Role of Joy

- **Scripture:** "Weeping may stay for the night, but rejoicing comes in the morning." — Psalm 30:5
- **Reflection:** Joy is a powerful force for healing and resilience.
- **Application:** Share something that brings you joy with someone else.

Day 364: The Importance of Trust

- **Scripture:** "Trust in the Lord with all your heart and lean not on your own understanding." — Proverbs 3:5-6
- **Reflection:** Trusting God enhances our resilience.

- **Application:** Reflect on an area where you need to trust God more.

Day 365: The Call to Action

- **Scripture:** "In the same way, faith by itself, if it is not accompanied by action, is dead." —James 2:17

- **Reflection:** Our faith should inspire action in nurturing others.

- **Application:** Identify a specific action you can take this week to nurture someone in your life.

About the Author

Rev. Dr. Anthony D. Allen, M.Div., BCC-MH, is a proud U.S. Army veteran, retired Chaplain, and Christian counselor with more than 30 years of experience in spiritual and mental health care. He is the Founder and CEO of Christ and Counseling 2 Consulting, LLC, and serves as Pastor of Tribe of Judah COGIC. He is also a member of Alpha Phi Alpha Fraternity, Inc.

A fifth-generation lifetime member of the Church of God in Christ, Dr. Allen has been recognized in the 2024–2025 *Marquis Who's Who in America* for his distinguished service in ministry, counseling, and leadership. He holds a Ph.D. in Counseling and Psychological Studies, a Master of Divinity, and a B.S. in Business Management. Board-certified by the National Association of Veterans Affairs Chaplains and a member of the American Association of Christian Counselors, Dr. Allen integrates faith, resilience, and evidence-based mental wellness across every sphere of life.